KU-166-970

www.dk.com

Editor Jane Yorke
Senior Editor Mary Atkinson
Art Editor Karen Lieberman
Senior Art Editor Chris Scollen
Designer Mary Sandberg
DTP Designer Phil Keeble
Production Josie Alabaster
Jacket Design Karen Lieberman
Picture Research Jamie Robinson
and Lee Thompson

Published in Great Britain by
Dorling Kindersley Limited
9 Henrietta Street
London WC2E 8PS

2 4 6 8 10 9 7 5 3 1

Copyright © 1999 Dorling Kindersley Limited, London
Text and concept copyright © 1999 Claire Llewellyn

All rights reserved. No part of this publication
may be reproduced, stored in a retrieval system,
or transmitted in any form or by any means, electronic,
mechanical, photocopying, recording, or otherwise,
without the prior written permission of the copyright owner.

A CIP catalogue record for this book is available
from the British Library.

ISBN: 0-7513-5849-5

Colour reproduction by Colourscan, Singapore
Printed and bound in Italy by L.E.G.O.

Contents

Land index

LAND

Discover the wonders of life on dry land

Claire Llewellyn

London • New York • Sydney • Moscow • Delhi

Rock makes the hard ground under our feet.

Rising high

In some parts of the world, rocks rise up to make towering mountain peaks.

A moun bear nee a warm fur coat.

4

Leap frog
A frog leaps to escape from danger or to catch a passing fly.

Land fact
A tiger has a stripy coat to help it hide in the forest or in long, dry grass.

Sea fact
A plaice has a blotchy, spotty skin to help it hide on the sea bed.

A gibbon's arms are longer than its legs.

Long toes help the gibbon to grab hold of branches.

Digging deep
Rabbits use their strong paws to dig burrows under the ground.

Trains, cars and bikes speed over the land.

The open road
Cars are fast and comfortable. They use bridges to get across rivers.

Bikes are driven by pedal power

Bike ride
A bike is cheap and easy to run, and it neve gets stuck in a jam.

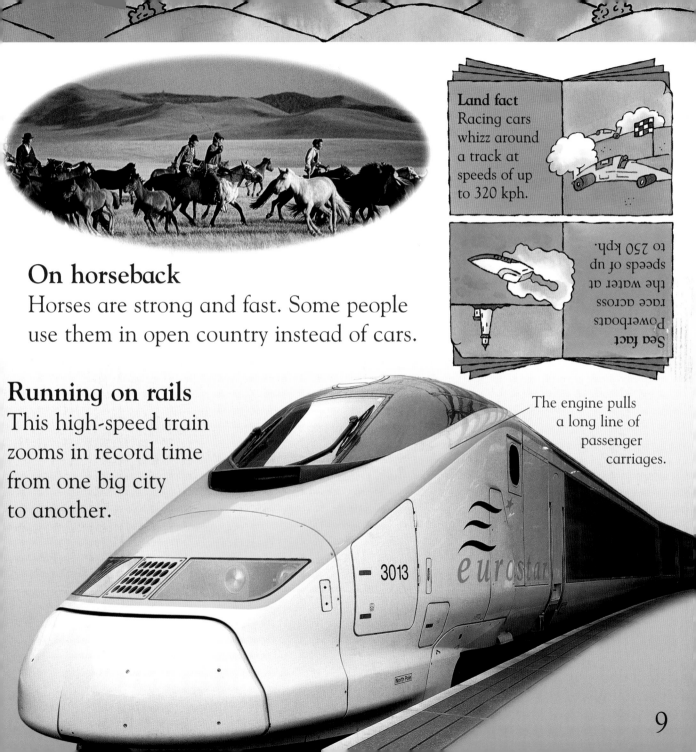

Land fact
Racing cars whizz around a track at speeds of up to 320 kph.

Sea fact
Powerboats race across the water at speeds of up to 250 kph.

On horseback

Horses are strong and fast. Some people use them in open country instead of cars.

Running on rails

This high-speed train zooms in record time from one big city to another.

The engine pulls a long line of passenger carriages.

3013

eurostar

Food crops grow in fertile soil.

Fruits of the Earth
Many plants grow sweet, juicy fruits that are good to eat.

Wheat crop
Wheat is the world's most important crop. The grains are use to make cereals, pasta, and bread.

10

A good harvest
A combine harvester holds enough wheat to make more than 7,000 loaves of bread.

Pretty horses
Most fish swim head first through the water, but seahorses swim upright.

Could a rabbit live in the salty sea?

No. A rabbit has lungs and can only breathe in air. It would drown under the sea.

Old rocks

This ancient leaf fossil, found inside a rock, is 25 million years old.

Great Reef

The Great Barrier Reef off Australia is 2,000 kilometres long.

Pearly shell

The shell of the tasty abalone is made into buttons and beads.

Pass the salt

We harvest salt from pools of seawater that are left to dry in the sun.

Sea fact
Coral reefs need protecting from the damage caused by divers and pollution.

Land fact
Rainforests are precious, yet many are cut down to clear land for farming.

Seaweed clings to rocks on the sea bed.

Seaweed goodness

Seaweed is full of good things. It is used in both foods and fertilisers.

Gemstones
Miners drill into rocks under the ground to find precious stones.

Land fact
Gold is a precious metal that is found in rocks under the ground.

Sea fact
Pearls are beads made of mother-of-pearl. They are found in certain shells.

A cut diamond

Timber!
Wood from tree trunks is used for building and to make furniture and paper.

Wheat grains

On top of the world

The land of Tibet is so high above sea level that it is called "the roof of the world".

Sea air

Divers carry tanks of air so that they can breathe under the water.

On the hoof
A horse gallops along on just two fingers and toes hidden inside hard, horny hooves.

Diving down
A submersible can dive three kilometres below the surface of the sea.

Could a fish survive on dry land?

No. A fish has gills and can only breathe in water. It would suffocate on dry land.

Lift the flaps to see the differences between the land and the sea.

Paddle power

Canoes have been used for transport for hundreds of years. Now these fast, light boats are also used for sport.

Sea fact
A lifeboat is used to rescue sailors in stormy seas and carry them to shore.

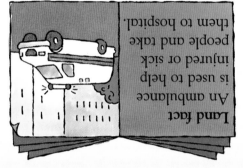

Land fact
An ambulance is used to help injured or sick people and take them to hospital.

Sailing along

A big sail catches enough wind to power a boat along.

Comfortable passenger cabins

The fruits of the sea give us good things to eat.

Fish are sorted and packed in ice.

Tasty catch
Lobsters are caught in lobster pots baited with scraps of fish.

Fishing fleet
Fishermen often face rough seas in the search for good catch of fish.

Small **boats** and mighty **ships** sail across the **oceans.**

Deep-sea diving
Scientists use a deep-sea submersible to dive down to the bottom of the sea.

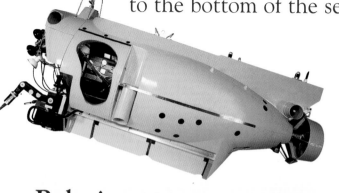

Relaxing at sea
Some people take their holiday at sea. They stay on luxury cruise ships that sail from port to port.

Suck and squirt
An octopus moves by sucking water into its baggy body and then squirting it out again very fast.

Sea fact
Many fish live in large groups, called shoals. A moving shoal is hard to attack.

Land fact
Zebras live in large groups, called herds. A herd is hard for a lion to attack.

Strong arms can open shells to reach the tasty shellfish inside.

World of fish
The sea is teeming with about 15,000 different kinds of fish.

Star crawler
Starfish creep and crawl over rocks, using tubes on the end of their arms.

Sea creatures **swim** with flippers and fins.

Diving dolphins
Dolphins spend their lives in the sea, but they come up to the surface to breathe.

Tiny tube feet

6

Sea of ice
Near the Poles the sea freezes over in winter, but slowly thaws in the spring.

Sea fact
Mountains rise up from the sea bed. The tallest peaks stick out of the sea.

Land fact
Mountains tower high above the land. Some of the tallest are covered in snow.

Surfers ride the breaking waves.

Wind and waves
Waves are made by strong winds blowing far out at sea.

Ocean waters are always on the move.

The salty sea
Most of the Earth is covered by sea. It laps around rocky coasts and on sandy beaches.

Coral reef
Rocky coral reefs are made by tiny animals in warm, sunlit seas

SEA

Explore the hidden world under the ocean

Claire Llewellyn

DK

London • New York • Sydney • Moscow • Delhi

Illustrated by Sally Kindberg

Photography by Max Alexander, Jane Burton, Peter Chadwick, Andy Crawford, Geoff Dann, Philip Dowell, Mike Dunning, Steve Gorton, Frank Greenaway, James Jackson, Colin Keates, Dave King, Richard Leeney, Ray Moller, Susanna Price, Tim Ridley, Tim Shepherd, Steve Shott, Harry Taylor, Andreas von Einsiedel, Jerry Young

The publisher would like to thank the following for their kind permission to reproduce their photographs:
a = above, c = centre, b = below/bottom, l = left, r = right, t = top.

Land
De Beers: 11tl; **Julian Cotton Photolibrary:** 3, 5br; **Robert Harding Picture Library:** Nik Wheeler 8tl; **Photonica:** G+J Fotoservice/ Ernst Wrba 5tl; **Pictor International:** 4c; **Tony Stone Images:** Stefan Reiss 6; Andy Sacks 10–11c; **Telegraph Colour Library:** V.C.L. 7l.

Sea
Britstock-IFA: 8–9b; AP&F/Rob Gilley 5br; **Bruce Coleman Ltd:** Nicholas de Vore 10–11c; **Exeter Maritime Museum:** 10–11ac; **Images Colour Library:** 9c, 10bl; **Tony Stone Images:** John Beatty 5tl; Chuck Davis 6c; Simeone Huber 4–5; **Telegraph Colour Library:** V.C.L. 3.

Gatefold
Planet Earth Pictures: Gary Bell lbc; Flip Schulke rbc; **Tibet Images:** Norma Joseph ltr.

Contents

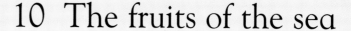

Sea index